CIVILIZATIONS OF THE WORLD

INCA CIVILIZATION

by Allison Lassieur

FOCUS
READERS

NAVIGATOR

WWW.FOCUSREADERS.COM

Focus Readers is distributed by North Star Editions:
sales@northstareditions.com | 888-417-0195

Produced for Focus Readers by Red Line Editorial.

Content Consultant: Michael A. Malpass, Professor of Anthropology, Ithaca College

Photographs ©: pnicolova/Shutterstock Images, cover, 1; ckchiu/Shutterstock Images, 4–5; Red Line Editorial, 7; OSTILL is Franck Camhi/Shutterstock Images, 8; Universal History Archive/UIG/Universal Images Group/Getty Images, 10–11; alessen/Shutterstock Images, 13; Ammit Jack/Shutterstock Images, 15; Martha Barreno/VWPics/AP Images, 16–17; Artokoloro Quint Lox Limited/Alamy, 19; World History Archive/Alamy, 21, 27; Enrique Castro-Mendivil/Reuters/Newscom, 22–23; worldroadtrip/Shutterstock Images, 25; Juan Karita/AP Images, 29

Library of Congress Cataloging-in-Publication Data
Names: Lassieur, Allison, author.
Title: Inca civilization / by Allison Lassieur.
Description: Lake Elmo, MN : Focus Readers, 2020. | Series: Civilizations of
  the world | Audience: Grade 4-6. | Includes bibliographical references and
  index.
Identifiers: LCCN 2018060599 (print) | LCCN 2018061391 (ebook) | ISBN
  9781641859653 (PDF) | ISBN 9781641858960 (ebook) | ISBN 9781641857581
  (hardcover) | ISBN 9781641858274 (pbk.)
Subjects: LCSH: Incas--Juvenile literature.
Classification: LCC F3429 (ebook) | LCC F3429 .L27 2020 (print) | DDC
  985/.019--dc23
LC record available at https://lccn.loc.gov/2018060599

Printed in the United States of America
Mankato, MN
May, 2019

ABOUT THE AUTHOR

Allison Lassieur is the author of more than 150 nonfiction books on history, science, culture, technology, and current events. She also writes novels, puzzle books, activity books, and games. She lives in upstate New York with her husband, daughter, three dogs, a cat, and more books than she can count.

TABLE OF CONTENTS

CHAPTER 1

City Builders 5

CHAPTER 2

Gods and Government 11

CHAPTER 3

Daily Life 17

CHAPTER 4

Important People 23

CONTRIBUTIONS

Freeze-Dried Food 28

Focus on Inca Civilization • 30
Glossary • 31
To Learn More • 32
Index • 32

CITY BUILDERS

Deep in the jungle, a city stands on the side of a mountain. Rows of houses and temples stretch between the peaks. These buildings are made from stacked blocks of stone. Long stone **terraces** stretch between them. Known as Machu Picchu, this city was built by the Incas.

Many Inca cities used stone terraces to create flat land for growing crops.

The Inca Empire stretched along the western edge of South America. At its height in 1533, the empire reached from modern-day Colombia all the way south to Chile. The empire was so big that the Incas divided it into four sections. They called their empire Tahuantinsuyu. This name means "the four parts together."

The Inca **civilization** began around 1200. The Incas started as a small group of people. They lived in the city of Cuzco. But they wanted more land and more power.

Around 1400, the Incas began to take over neighboring tribes. During the next 100 years, more and more tribes came under Inca control. Many disliked their Inca rulers. The Incas often took people from their homes and forced them to work far away. Some people tried to fight back. But the Incas continued to expand.

INCA EXPANSION

COLOMBIA
ECUADOR
BRAZIL
PERU
Cuzco
Lake Titicaca
BOLIVIA
CHILE
ARGENTINA

- 1438–1463
- 1463–1471
- 1471–1493
- 1493–1525

Inca nobles might have worn clothing similar to what this man is wearing.

By 1530, they ruled more than seven million people.

For many years, the Incas had the largest empire in South America. That began to change in 1532. That year, Spanish **conquistadors** arrived in search of gold. The Spanish fought against the Incas. They kidnapped and killed

Inca rulers. They also brought deadly diseases, such as smallpox. Conquered people joined the Spanish to fight against the Incas. Eventually, the Inca Empire collapsed.

FINDING MACHU PICCHU

For years, the locations of Inca cities were unknown to people outside of Peru. Explorers from other countries sometimes tried to find them. Hiram Bingham was an adventurer from the United States. He led a group to Peru in 1911. They were searching for a city in the Andes Mountains. A local farmer told them about some ruins. The ruins turned out to be Machu Picchu. News of this discovery spread quickly around the world. People could now learn more about the Incas.

CHAPTER 2

GODS AND GOVERNMENT

The Incas referred to their emperor as the Sapa Inca. He lived in the capital city of Cuzco. The Sapa Inca was an absolute ruler. Everything in the empire belonged to him. His word was law. The Incas believed he was a **descendant** of the sun god, Inti. They treated him with great honor and respect.

Huayna Capac was a Sapa Inca who ruled from 1493 to 1525.

Thousands of nobles served under the Sapa Inca. They gave him advice and helped him run the empire. Being a noble was a great honor. Nobles enjoyed wealth and comfort. The Sapa Inca gave them land and servants. Every noble wore an ear **ornament**. These ornaments made it easy for other people to identify them as government officials.

Four governors reported directly to the Sapa Inca. Each governor was in charge of one section of the empire. Other nobles ruled smaller towns and villages. These nobles made sure the local people followed Inca law. Breaking the law had serious consequences. The punishment

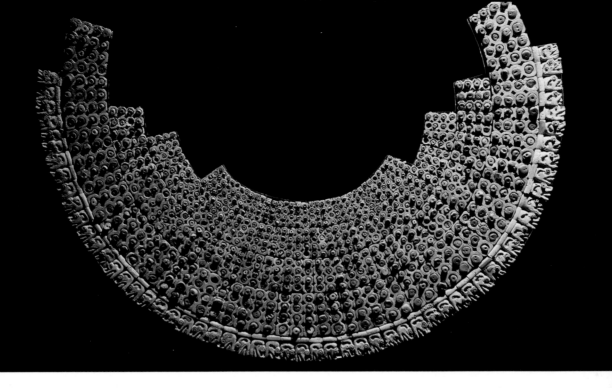

Inca nobles often wore gold jewelry.

for crimes such as stealing or murder could be death.

Towns and villages were made up of groups called ayllus. An ayllu was a small group of families. Several ayllus lived and worked together in a village. They grew food or provided labor for the empire.

Religion was another important part of Inca life. The two most powerful gods were Viracocha and Inti. But the Incas worshipped many gods and goddesses. Many were based on nature. Illapa was the god of thunder and rain. Mama Quilla was the goddess of the moon.

CHILDREN OF THE SUN

The Incas believed Viracocha created the world. Afterward, he traveled to Lake Titicaca in the Andes Mountains. There, he created the sun, moon, animals, and people. He gave each group of people their own **culture**. The Incas had a special relationship with the god Inti. They believed he protected them and helped their crops grow. They called themselves the "children of the sun."

The Temple of the Sun at Ingapirca, Ecuador, was built from stones fitted together without mortar.

The Incas worked to honor and **appease** the gods. They built **sacred** sites throughout their empire. Priests held religious ceremonies at these places. They left offerings of food and drink. The Incas also prayed the gods would not cause earthquakes or storms.

CHAPTER 3

DAILY LIFE

People in the Inca Empire were divided by ranks, or levels of power and importance. The Sapa Inca was at the top. The noble class came next. At the bottom were the commoners. These people worked as farmers, artists, and craftsmen. They lived in simple homes made of mud bricks and stone.

A replica shows the kind of mud home Incas likely lived in.

All commoners belonged to ayllus. These groups were organized based on families. People in each ayllu worked together. Some were farmers. They grew crops such as potatoes, corn, squash, beans, and peppers. They also built warehouses to store the food.

Other commoners worked as artists or craftsmen. The best artists worked for the Sapa Inca. But artists also made objects used in daily life. Women wove fabric with colorful, detailed designs. Even simple clay bowls and cups were highly decorated.

Sometimes the Sapa Inca ordered new roads or temples to be built. The nobles

The Incas often made ceramic jars with round bodies and long necks.

would order the commoners to do those jobs. Commoners did not get paid for their work. In fact, people kept only one-third of what they made or grew. They had to give the other two-thirds to the government.

Officials collected the food and goods. They stored some in huge warehouses. They sent the rest to other parts of the empire. Leaders in those areas would give it out to people who needed it. In this way, different parts of the Inca Empire worked together. Their leaders made

SHINING LIKE THE SUN

Most Inca art was made of gold. Because this metal is shiny, it was associated with the sun god. Artists made gold and silver statues for the temples. They also crafted golden cups, plates, and jewelry. Unfortunately, few of these objects exist today. Spanish explorers stole most of them and melted them down to make gold and silver coins.

Sculptures of alpacas and llamas were made from stone and gold and left as offerings for the gods.

sure that everyone had enough food and goods to survive.

This system of sharing was quite successful. If one area had a problem, such as a bad crop, other areas could help. In fact, the Incas did not use money. Sometimes people would barter, or trade goods for other goods. But in general, they already had what they needed.

IMPORTANT PEOPLE

According to legend, the Incas' first ruler was Manco Capac. Several myths describe how he founded the city of Cuzco. However, he may not have been a real person.

Many historians believe it was the Incas' ninth ruler who founded the Inca Empire. His name was Pachacuti.

Actors portray the legend of Manco Capac.

Pachacuti was the ninth Sapa Inca. He ruled from 1438 to 1471. As a young man, Pachacuti defended Cuzco from nearby enemies. He and his descendants conquered many neighboring tribes. Under their rule, the Incas built a network of stone roads to connect their cities.

FOUNDING CUZCO

In one legend, Manco Capac had a golden staff. Inti told him to travel until the staff sank easily into the ground. There, he would build a great city. Manco Capac searched the Andes Mountains until he found a beautiful valley. His staff sank, so he built a city there. The legend says Manco Capac also created the Incas' first laws.

Ruins of the city of Pisac still exist in Peru.

Their huge cities and forts spread far beyond Cuzco.

Stories of great cities filled with gold reached all the way to Europe. The Spanish wanted the gold for themselves. So, in 1532, a group of soldiers went to Peru. Led by Francisco Pizarro, they came upon the Inca city of Cajamarca.

The Incas' ruler, Atahuallpa, was staying near the city. He tried to capture the Spanish. But they captured him instead. Atahuallpa offered Pizarro a room full of gold in exchange for his freedom. Pizarro took the gold. But he refused to let the Inca leader go. A few months later, Pizarro killed Atahuallpa. Then he began taking over the Inca Empire.

Pizarro and his men marched from city to city. They easily defeated the large Inca armies. The Spanish soldiers had guns and armor. They also brought diseases that the Incas had never faced before. These diseases killed thousands of Incas. The Spanish also had help from

Atahuallpa fought in a civil war from 1525 to 1532 to become Sapa Inca.

the conquered people. Several tribes joined the fight against the Incas. By 1572, the Incas could no longer resist. Their empire was no more. However, they left behind great cities. Their influence lives on in the people who live in South America today.

FREEZE-DRIED FOOD

A French scientist found a way to freeze-dry food in 1906. But he was not the first person to use this process. The Incas had used a method for freeze-drying hundreds of years earlier.

The Inca Empire covered thousands of square miles. People often traveled long distances. They carried food with them. But they needed a way to keep it from spoiling. Freeze-drying was the perfect answer. This process **preserves** food. In this process, food is frozen and thawed. Then, melted water is pressed out of the food.

The ancient Incas often freeze-dried potatoes. This food was called *chuño*. The Incas froze the potatoes in snow from the Andes Mountains. Then they placed the potatoes in the sun to thaw. They

People in the Andes Mountains still make *chuño* today.

stomped on the food as it thawed. This action pressed all the water out. The dried food stayed good for much longer than usual. A freeze-dried potato could be stored for years.

FOCUS ON
INCA CIVILIZATION

Write your answers on a separate piece of paper.

1. Write a paragraph describing Pachacuti's role in the history of the Inca Empire.

2. What are the advantages of a society in which everyone works together to produce and share goods? Can you think of any disadvantages?

3. What was the name of the Inca sun god?
   A. Inti
   B. Illapa
   C. Mama Quilla

4. How did disease help the Spanish take over South America?
   A. As more people became sick, the Incas' weapons were less effective.
   B. As more people became sick, more Incas joined the side of the Spanish.
   C. As more people became sick, fewer Incas could fight back against the invaders.

Answer key on page 32.

GLOSSARY

appease
To keep someone calm or happy, often by giving a gift.

civilization
A large group of people with a shared history, culture, and form of government.

conquistadors
People from Spain and Portugal who took over land in Central and South America in the 1500s.

culture
The way people live; their customs, beliefs, and laws.

descendant
Someone who comes from a particular family, ancestor, or group of people.

ornament
A small object worn as jewelry or used for decorating.

preserves
Treats food to prevent it from going bad.

sacred
Having spiritual or religious meaning.

terraces
Groups of long, flat areas along a mountainside created by building walls.

TO LEARN MORE

BOOKS

Garbe, Suzanne. *Secrets of Machu Picchu: Lost City of the Incas*. North Mankato, MN: Capstone Press, 2015.

Nussbaum, Ben. *Inka Terraces*. Huntington Beach, CA: Teacher Created Materials, 2019.

Weitzman, Elizabeth. *Mysteries of Machu Picchu*. Minneapolis: Lerner Publications, 2018.

NOTE TO EDUCATORS

Visit **www.focusreaders.com** to find lesson plans, activities, links, and other resources related to this title.

INDEX

Andes Mountains, 9, 14, 24, 28
Atahuallpa, 26
ayllus, 13, 18

chuño, 28–29
conquistadors, 8
Cuzco, 6–7, 11, 23–25

gold, 8, 20, 25–26

Illapa, 14
Inti, 11, 14, 20, 24

Machu Picchu, 5, 9
Mama Quilla, 14
Manco Capac, 23–24

Pachacuti, 23–24
Pizarro, Francisco, 25–26
potatoes, 18, 28–29

Sapa Inca, 11–12, 17–18, 24
smallpox, 9

Tahuantinsuyu, 6
temples, 5, 18, 20

Viracocha, 14

Answer Key: 1. Answers will vary; **2.** Answers will vary; **3.** A; **4.** C